ENGAGEMENT WHISPERER

A catalogue record for this book is available from the National Library of Australia.

ISBN: 978-0-648189-20-6

Editor: Desolie Page

Cover Design by c8v_logos on Fiverr.com

Internal formatting by Mark Thomas / coverness.com

ENGAGEMENT WHISPERER

A QUIETER AND MORE COLLABORATIVE APROACH TO INSPIRING YOUR TEAM

Dr TRACY STANLEY

ENGAGEMENTWHISPERER.COM

Table of Contents

Advance Praise for Engagement Whisperer

Dr Stanley's book is a valuable resource for managers in large organisations as it reveals the characteristics that most engage people and provides practical advice on how we can create the conditions to bring out the best in our employees.

Dr Monique Beedles, *Managing Director, Teak Yew*

*

Tracy cleverly brings together the essential dos and don'ts for creating engaging workplaces.

A must read for managers who want to get the best out of their teams – and themselves!

Huibert Evekink, *CEO Futureteaming and Author of Feedback First*

There are lots of gems to be found in 'Engagement Whisperer'. If all managers followed the advice given in each of the easy to read chapters, the corporate world would be a lot happier and more satisfying place for everyone.

'Engagement Whisperer' is a must read for anyone who manages people. It's conversational, easy to read style delivers some fundamental messages for valuing staff and bringing out their best. The practical list of actions to do and to avoid at the end of each chapter are great 'take home' (or rather take to work) messages.

Cathy Turner, *Business Analyst, Australian Government Agency*

*

This is an enjoyable and thoughtful book on a difficult topic that is forever present in an organisation. The layout and structure makes it very accessible and it will help the reader reflect on their own experiences while identifying areas where they can take steps to enhance the engagement of their team.

Michael Connell, *Executive General Manager Southern Region, Silver Chef*

This thoughtful and practical book dispels the myths that 'engagement' happens because of glitzy, once a year initiatives. It's a relief for those who can't offer curated workspaces complete with ping pong tables, free lattes and bean bags adorning the ubiquitous 'chill out zones' where the magic happens!

Tracy's work shows that real and sustained engagement comes from a more thoughtful and human centred place: a place where respect, trust, fairness and personal growth sit at the core. Engagement is now demystified and accessible to all. It should come with a product warning: putting these changes into practice may bring you under the spotlight. Expect to be asked for your recipe for team success - or leave your peers secretly wondering if there is something in the water!

Wendy Lundgaard, *Principal Consultant/CEO of Win-Win Workplace Strategies*

I dedicate this book to all managers seeking to inspire their team to be their best

Why a Whisperer?

In a world where we are bombarded by *shouty* messages, I wanted to write a quiet book. To whisper the simple messages I learnt about engaging your team.

'Whisperer'– as revealed by Google

whisperer

noun

1. a person who whispers.

"he's a whisperer—you can hardly hear a word he says"

2. a person skilled in taming or training a specified kind of animal, typically using body language and gentle vocal encouragement rather than physical contact.

"he's reportedly set to quit show business to become a horse whisperer"

Also …

Whisperer – Definition by the Free Dictionary – www.freedictionary.com/whisperer

1. Soft speech produced without using the full voice
2. Something uttered very softly: overheard his whisper
3. A secretly or …

Engagement Whisperer

How many 'Whisperers' have you heard of? If you are an over 40, Robert Redford in the movie 'Horse Whisperer' may have been the first whisperer to come to mind. A romantic movie with tragedy, horses (of course) and Robert Redford, aka 'The Horse Whisperer', a man who quietly weaves his magic to restore a horse and a relationship.

If you work in academia, you may have heard of the 'Thesis Whisperer', a blog nurtured by Inger Mewburn who has become the 'Thesis Whisperer'. She helps struggling students combat imposter syndrome and the challenge of getting that 'darn thesis' done.

I like the term 'Whisperer' because of the sense of quiet wisdom and a 'softly, softly' approach. This is why I called this book 'Engagement Whisperer'.

ENTREE

*T*hanks for dropping by.

I want this book to be like your favourite café: a comfy place where you could drop in, take a break and pick up nourishing takeaways, such as useful ideas (or carrot cake) to improve your team's engagement.

The book is divided into six generous slices – I mean sections.

In the first slice, I talk about how I gathered information about employee engagement, developed insights and then wrote it all down.

Then I spend a bit of time talking about the main ingredients that make a great job such as autonomy, learning opportunity and solving challenging problems.

In the third slice, I talk about working with others in teams. There's a lot to say about the power of collaboration, interactive meetings, good relationships and feeling supported.

The fourth slice looks at what the best managers do, highlighting the importance of being open to new ideas, providing recognition and making team members feel valued. The relationship you have with your team members will have a big impact on their (and your) engagement.

In the fifth slice, we look at the reality of working in a big organisation, and how it influences our sense of who we are and how connected we feel.

Finally, for the last slice of cake we pull it all together. We listen to HR managers talking about their experiences in driving employee engagement initiatives. Big organisations tend to use big programs to enhance engagement. Employee engagement programs all come from a good place with some being implemented more effectively than others. I have combined the best of what my HR colleagues shared was important for success. If you are rolling out an organisational-wide initiative I trust you will find their insights of value.

Best wishes,
Tracy

1

Why the interest in employee engagement?

L ike many who have worked in large corporations I have experienced the joy of being deeply engaged in my work (so that time flies by) and the despair of not. These opposing experiences piqued my interest in employee engagement. The topic was discussed frequently in human resources journals with impressive claims being made about the relationship between engaged employees and improved business outcomes.

Being in human resources gave me opportunity to implement programs and processes to measure engagement (whatever we thought that was) and then to help managers do something useful with the findings: to take tangible steps to increase engagement within their team.

This process was a rich learning experience. While we – 'we' being the HR team – gathered valuable information about how the workplace was perceived, implementing a process to positively drive change was hard. Really hard. Expectations that change would follow the data collection process had been created. Reasonably so. Everyone's expectations were different. Some thought that changes to human resource policy and practice were key in lifting engagement. Increasing everyone's pay was often mentioned as the panacea for solving widespread disengagement. I was always sceptical of this view.

Before I go further it's important to explain my earlier comment about the definition of employee engagement. The term was introduced by Kahn in 1990, and has been used extensively by consultants and academics. Controversy followed, with some arguing that it has a duplication of meaning with earlier, and now less fashionable, concepts such as job satisfaction or job involvement or organisational commitment. Since then many pages have been devoted to discussing what it is and indeed what it isn't.

I need to do this as well.

For the purposes of my research, I defined employee

engagement as the multiple emotional, rational and behavioural dimensions of an employee's consistent level of effort, commitment and connection to their job. Yes, I know that this is a tad long-winded and academic. When I spoke to different employees, I explained it in the following way:

'Being highly engaged is when you are very absorbed in your work, you put your "heart into it" and exert a lot of energy to succeed.'

Let me give this definition more meaning by revisiting what 'work' is.

Discussing the concept of work is probably another book in itself. Needless to say how we feel and think about the things that we do when we exchange labour for money, influences how we behave when we're 'on the job'. Engagement has these three core components: feeling, thinking and acting. They are all connected to each other, with feelings and thoughts influencing behaviour and vice versa.

So, my definition is very much related to the job that you are doing. Through my research I found that engagement exists on many levels. An employee develops a complex relationship with the organisation, with their manager and with their team, a relationship that's separate from their feeling of attachment or not, as the case may be, to the work they are doing.

Throughout my career I have been involved in measuring and enhancing engagement and have learnt a great deal through these activities. It was interesting that while we collected useful information, my overriding impression was that there was an over-reliance on 'fixing' problems in team processes as the remedy for low engagement. While this was an important part of the engagement jigsaw puzzle it was only one part. I knew that being engaged was also related to me, to my objectives for work, the culture of my team and my integration within it and how I felt about the direction and values of the organisation.

Why I wanted to learn more about Employee Engagement

I wanted to learn more about engagement for three reasons. Selfishly I guess, I was interested in examining those times and those conditions when I was most engaged in an organisation. Also of interest was learning from other people's experiences so that I could identify the common characteristics that supported engagement. From this knowledge, I wanted to develop tools and resources that everyone and especially managers could use to create the right conditions for engagement.

My research revealed that while there was a complexity of things in the workplace (and at home) that influenced engagement at work, it wasn't rocket science. I wanted to demystify this and prepare guidelines that anyone

managing people could use to enhance their employees'
engagement at work.

2

How I collected stories about employee engagement

Taking a sabbatical from corporate life to undertake a PhD gave me the opportunity to learn more about employee engagement. A global, employee-owned, multi-disciplinary, professional services firm employing 11,000 people kindly let me in to investigate how a work environment influences employee engagement. A work environment was a broad concept including job-related factors, team processes and team climate, manager behaviours and physical environment elements.

While this is not a large sample, I think the findings

are interesting and potentially useful for others working in large organisations.

Over a six-month period I had access to five teams undertaking engineering, analytic, marketing and finance operations activities. I interviewed forty employees in total and observed eight team meetings. This involved a fair bit of waiting in the reception and wandering around the offices – all of which provided insight into the organisation's culture.

A semi-structured interview process provided a consistent approach to collecting information about engagement while granting flexibility to explore things that popped up during these conversations.

So, my findings about employee engagement come from inside this organisation, combined with my own experience as a human resource practitioner. I have also sought the advice of human resources specialists, tapping into their experience in running employee engagement programs and lessons learned. This experience has helped me to suggest processes and tools to help employees, managers and human resources professionals take steps to enhance engagement.

My approach is influenced by a belief in the value of a 'softly, softly' approach to enhancing engagement – hence the title, 'Engagement Whisperer'. There is already so much noise in organisations that a quieter approach might just be the right 'cup of tea.'

(Please note all names used in this book are pseudonyms, that is they're fake, although the quotes are real).

3

Big Picture –
What did I learn?

Well, in a nutshell, a great deal.

The major finding was that there are many characteristics in a work environment that interact in a complex and cumulative manner to influence employee engagement. And this is before you consider the many influences on the employees themselves such as motivation, personality and life circumstances.

Engagement is clearly experienced on multiple levels and is subject to change. These levels are with your job, with your team, with your manager and with your organisation. And depending upon what is happening in your life at any particular point, some aspects will engage you more than others.

So, there's not a simple answer to the question of how a work environment influences employee engagement.

And while there are common things that pretty much everyone values, some aspects of the work environment are valued more highly by some, than others.

Let's talk a little bit more about work …

4

The nature of work

W̲e spend a lot of our time 'at work' in a 'job'. But what is a job?

This is a really good question as the nature of work is changing with new jobs emerging with delicious titles such as a Social Media Ninja, Fashion Evangelist, Hacker-in-Residence, or Chief Happiness Officer.

For my amusement and between mouthfuls I googled 'What is a job?'

A common definition appearing at the top of the search list was

'A task or piece of work for which one undertakes for pay'.

A grossly unhelpful description.

A slightly more useful definition came from dictionary.com:

'A group of homogenous tasks related by similarity of functions. When performed by an employee in exchange for pay, a job consists of duties, responsibilities and tasks (performance elements) that are defined and specific and can be accomplished quantified measured and rated'.

Whoa. Goodness this is dry – and perhaps not reflecting the evolving nature of many jobs.

I then clicked on synonyms for 'job' in MS Word and was offered occupation, trade, profession, career and of course 'work'. These terms reveal the way we have traditionally looked at a job – as a trade, a profession or as a stepping stone on a career path.

So, to pull together the essence of a job, it consists of:

'A collection of activities that are undertaken to achieve certain objectives in return for pay and other benefits.'

In large organisations these benefits are often related to learning and career evolution. Big organisations have hundreds of these 'collections of activities' which often become part of a job description. So, that is the definition I am going to run with in this book.

Having clarified what a job is, let's look at the characteristics of a job that most contribute to engagement from an employee's perspective.

I mean – let's eat our first slice of cake…

JOBS

5

Challenging jobs stretch us and bring out our best

Tough challenges force employees to think and work harder. A challenge in their job could take many forms: solving a nutty problem, introducing a new system, or working with stakeholders with competing interests. These challenges typically get your employee's brain sparking as they try to find the solution. To respond to the challenge, the employee draws on existing knowledge and seeks new knowledge from other sources such as other people or web based sources like Google.

Here are examples of times when employees felt stretched:

The bigger challenges in our projects – these are the

projects when I need to do my best thinking. John

We don't have enough hours in the system or they've got more or we've got more or the rate's changed and we haven't been informed and it hasn't been updated. It's, yeah, it's fun. I actually do enjoy it. I like getting to the bottom of things. Lisa

What I like in my work is when I do technical things and I find some technical-minded solutions. You know? And things like that. I'm a technocrat. I'm an engineer first and a manager maybe later. Terry

These challenges extend an employee's thinking, help them develop analytical and interpersonal skills and contribute to feelings of engagement.

Many people like to learn. Solving problems can energise us and bring out our best thinking. It's not surprising that when our job stops challenging us we might look around for a new one.

So, what steps can you take to include more challenge in your employee's job?

To DO

- Talk to your employees about developing their role and where they want to develop skills.
- Build more complex tasks into their roles over time.

- Suggest a new project or short-term assignment where they can develop specific skills valued by the organisation or employee and work with people from different professional or cultural backgrounds.
- Delegate projects with broader scope and complexity.
- Encourage them to apply for a bigger job. Discuss options with them as a part of a career development conversation: show your confidence in their growing capabilities.
- Propose a job swap.
- Seek ways to automate routine aspects of their role.

To AVOID

- Solving the problem or challenge for them.
- Keeping them in a role with little opportunity to learn new things – unless that is what they want at that time.
- Pushing them into a role that they are not equipped to succeed in.

6

Learning and mastering a skill is a wonderful and empowering thing

A logical extension of problem solving is learning. It will surprise no one that engaged employees love to learn. Learning can come when we are working on our own, thinking deeply about a problem or when we're discussing the problem with others. These are often the times when we're most 'in the zone'.

The opportunity to learn and master new skills is key for progressing in organisations. Your team members with potential and motivation to take on broader roles will be keen to learn new skills to help them to step up. Having conversations with these team members about the skills they want to acquire and the best way of doing this, is an important part of your role as a leader Encourage their self-reflection and action planning to move them in the direction of their career aspirations. Ask questions about when and where they learn best so they can create the best conditions for facilitating learning.

Here are examples of times when the people I spoke with were in that 'learning zone'.

When I'm really sitting down and looking at a problem and I'm not sure what the solution could be and you might have an idea. And you often go into those trances where you are thinking – will this work? – yeah – where you are just thinking about your problem. It often happens because there are a lot of complicated things that are happening. Wallace

We had a problem to solve for a client and there were a few guys quite similar in experience. We discussed longer than we actually worked on it, but it came out a very good result. Terry

I suppose we bounce ideas off each other and say: Do you have this problem when doing this? Is there any way? Has anyone thought of …? Have you got that problem and how did you cope with that? Marie

As a manager think about where the richest learning opportunities come from in your team. For example, do they come from new projects, from boisterous conversations, from reflection or from spending time investigating how others have approached a similar challenge? If you model a curiosity in seeking to understand a situation, they are likely to follow your lead. Another useful way to help your team is to ask questions like:

- Can you remember a time at work when you were learning a great deal?
- Where were you?
- What was happening?
- How were you feeling?

Then lead the conversation around how we can create more of these opportunities for them, and for other members in the team.

Additionally, at the end of a project encourage your team to take time out, to eat cake and to reflect on what worked and what didn't. Documenting 'lessons learned' will be a useful resource for the future and perhaps for other teams facing similar challenges.

Discussing learning from failure destigmatises it and creates greater openness and trust within the team. Encourage your team members to write down their learning, perhaps on a napkin or in a private journal. This is a useful way for them to mentor themselves and keep a record of their progress. At other times employing an external coach might be the best option.

As they develop confidence and take responsibility for addressing their knowledge gaps, remind them of the value of letting colleagues know about what they are trying to learn and where they want to go in their career. Other people have insights and access to people and resources that could help your team members build their skills.

Be aware that asking for help is a skill some lack. It's a confidence thing. You may need to show them how to reach out if they're unsure.

Try nibbling on these ...

To DO

- Display and encourage curiosity. (For example, what are the delicious ingredients in this cake?)
- Discuss lessons learned when the team gets together.
- Provide feedback and positive guidance to support their learning.
- Encourage them to keep a learning journal to track their progress in building their skills.
- Create opportunities for employees to work together on projects or when trying to solve a problem.

To AVOID

- Not encouraging employees to reflect on learning from activities.

7

Autonomy is a staple of life – Give your team members freedom

This finding will surprise no one. Many researchers before me have reported how important autonomy is, particularly if you have a bit of experience. Autonomy contributes to engagement in the same way that cream-cheese frosting boosts the taste of carrot cake! People love freedom: freedom to decide when and how work will be undertaken. Autonomy and freedom are all about having control, self-expression and the power to drive your work in the direction you think best. It's also about the freedom to make mistakes. It's an absolute 'food staple' in engaging your employees.

Here are a few reflections from a few people who shared their stories with me:

If I want to do something – I can just do it. There are no show stoppers. You can do it. It's essentially up to you. John

He (my manager) really understands that and is letting me go off to do what I really need to do … We are super autonomous in what we do. Sally

Notably, the importance of autonomy to engagement was more apparent when discussing feelings of disengagement, the very opposite of engaged:

My manager is good in the sense that she doesn't micro manage and I've had previous jobs where I have been micro-managed to the 't' … and sometimes I was just like wow – let it go. Like a two sentence memo that I had to send out she would completely rewrite it and I thought – just write it yourself then. Joan

So, as a manager don't forget Elsa's famous words of liberation from 'Frozen', *Let it go.* Give your employees freedom to decide how to undertake their work, with the exception perhaps being for junior employees who may need more direction. Let them keep the 'training wheels on their bicycle' until they feel confident to ride off unassisted.

So, to recap …

To DO

- Establish high-level expectations and then leave employees free to determine how to meet them.
- Give them space.

To AVOID

- Anything that whiffs of micro managing. For example, checking in too frequently.

8

It feels great to achieve things – even little things

Jobs have different activities and objectives. The job could be one big project or many smaller tasks. Being able to put a tick on a To Do list or write the words DONE on a project status document gives a buzz of accomplishment. It feels great to achieve things, even little things.

As these moments can often be fleeting it's important not to miss them in the daily hustle and bustle of a work day. Help your team members to note and celebrate these milestones – even if they are only petit-fours or mini moments. Petit-fours are powerful (a petit-four is a posh French word for a small fancy cake – just a bite sized morsel).

Examples of times when those interviewed experienced a sense of accomplishment included:

When you've got a good job where you don't have anything that's going to hold you up, where you can just be powering through it and everything is just running well, but also you're feeling busy and that you're accomplishing something. Ralph

At the end of the day you're able to help people with tasks that they don't do every day, that's not their main task in their role. And they're able to go away feeling that they've accomplished something. I feel like I've given them the best customer service I can. Marie

Even though like it was probably some of the longest weeks I've worked – well and truly, it was six and a half days a week kind of thing … which were long days. You were working towards something and the people around you were generally sort of appreciating that. James

As a manager you can do things to make sure your employee's coffee and cake come together. In management speak this is ensuring that achievement and recognition are enjoyed at the same time. Here are a few ideas …

To DO

• Provide opportunities for employees to have responsibility for, and to achieve, complete pieces of work.

• Help your staff to identify milestone moments in their work. When they achieve these, take the opportunity to say well done in person, in an email, in front of their peers, or all of the above. For bigger achievements, a bigger slice of cake (type of recognition) may be in order.

• Ask your staff members, 'What can I do to help you to be (more) successful today?'

To AVOID

• The opposite of above: forgetting your employee's major (and sometimes their mini) milestones.

9

We all want to be recognised

Everyone, and I mean everyone, regardless of how much experience they have appreciates a quiet nod or a few words of appreciation in recognition for a job well done. It's like a super energy bar, adding a spring to your step. However, recognition moments can be easily missed in the busy-busy daily thrust of attending meetings, participating in phone calls and writing reports. A timely moment for a positive shout-out to a staff member can easily pass while everyone is on the daily treadmill of emails and presentations. As a manager, it's important that you don't miss these moments.

For big achievements, create more 'applause', aligning

this with what the recipient would value. For example, you could provide recognition in a public meeting or via a letter from a senior manager or the chief executive officer. If you know your team members well, you will be able to pick the right way to give recognition.

It's hard to overstate how important recognition is. In a large organisation it's possible to feel lost and invisible. Being recognised is a sign that you are valued. And we all want to be valued. Knowing that the things you do are appreciated makes a big difference to how you feel in showing up for work each day. And make it specific: be clear what the individual is being recognised for. Avoid references to 'great job today' vs 'the way you handled that (specific) customer call you took before lunch was exceptional. Well done!'

Here's how recognition can power your team along:

You were working towards something and the people around you were generally sort of appreciating that or sort of realising that you were putting in that bit extra. James

When you get good feedback from others, that's probably the best feeling I think. And then you work better afterwards, after receiving that feedback. Nigel

Being asked to go over there and to work was huge to me. That was recognition of my experience. Madelene

Providing recognition is such an easy thing to do, using words and actions.

So summarising the good stuff on recognition …

To DO

- Provide timely recognition for your team members' achievements in a way they value.
- Look for behaviour to recognise in all the team members over time.
- Celebrate big when the opportunity presents itself.
- Don't forget colleagues or internal clients – they also value a positive word. In fact, the more we give recognition and say thanks, the more this behaviour becomes a valued part of the way things get done in the organisation. Over time these behaviours can positively shape the culture.

To AVOID

- Missing an opportunity to say *well done* or *good on you*. Obviously.
- Singling out the same individuals for recognition and ignoring others – note that we are prone to notice people who operate like ourselves. There is value in a variety of approaches and no 'one best way' of doing things

10

A little bit of time pressure gives us focus ... even though we groan

Time pressure is a curious thing. While a looming deadline provides focus, too much pressure can be demotivating: we feel we have failed before we've even started. Clearly a sweet spot exists: just the right amount of *chocolate sprinkles on the cupcake* to balance time pressures.

I'm a strong believer that work expands to fill available time. If a job has to be done in ten minutes, it will get done in ten minutes. If you have ten days, it will take ten days. Sure, what gets delivered in ten minutes is likely to be less than what is delivered in ten days. However, the time pressure will have driven a laser-sharp focus on what is really important. The result after ten minutes may be 80% there.

But don't just believe me. Listen to a few, wise words from other people working in an organisation.

I love working under pressure. Probably that is a bit of personality thing ... Because I am committed to pushing myself – I enjoy situations where we are challenged. From projects we have done there is no better feeling than handing over the keys to a plant that you have designed and built. Milos

I would have to say sort of end of financial year, that's a time where I'm really into and focussed on my work. When I have to meet sort of a deadline and things need to be done, I sort of focus and put my headphones in and sort of drown everything else out. Heather

I suppose when you are not as busy – you are a bit disengaged – like I said before I feel like I get less done when I am less stressed. So I am probably a bit more disengaged when I am not as busy. Alice

One aspect is time. If I'm given enough time, normally I perform a little better. I can't really think when it's time

pressure – looking at the next five minutes and the next 10 minutes. But too much time is also not very good (laughs); just the right amount of time. Jorge

Have you heard of the Pomodoro Technique? It recommends removing all distractions and working in timed intervals during the day, say of 30 minutes each spaced out by short breaks of five minutes. This process and the self-imposed time pressure help to keep focus on the task. If you want to learn more, google 'Pomodoro Technique' – at the time of writing I found the Wikipedia page a good place to start.

So, topping up your tea …

To DO

- Provide timeframes for activities which both push your employee to get going while providing enough time to explore alternative ways to approach the task.
- Discuss with them how much time this might be.
- Encourage them to try the Pomodoro Technique for a week and report back on how it went. Idea: If they have a report to write suggest they set a timer for 20 minutes and don't stop writing for anything short of a nuclear war.
- If they don't have a deadline set one for them.
- Ensure the right amount of 'work' so that they are fully occupied and motivated.

To AVOID

- Providing unrealistic, imposed timeframes. (If team members have a say in an unrealistic timeframe it is more likely to be met.)
- Giving too much work so that your employee feels overloaded.

*

Having looked at job-related influences on engagement, let's have a squiz at the many characteristics within your team environment, which also influence a person's sense of engagement.

TEAMS

There's a lot to say about teams. And many people have. Indeed, they have invested multiple pages extolling their virtues Why? High powered teams are the engine for getting things done in organisations. A great team can be the reason people stay in a less than stimulating job and invest high levels of energy. For many people, it is the team environment that has the biggest impact on their engagement – a bit like the baking powder in the cake. It makes the cake rise.

I'm going to chat about collaborative teams, the power of good relationships, being able to be open, feeling supported, feeling safe to say what you think and make a mistake, and I'm going to *wax lyrical* about what happens when you have a meeting, a really good meeting. (I know that we all have experiences of boring ones that waste our time). And I'm also going to touch on things you can do to fire up virtual or remote teams.

11

A collaborative team works and feels better

Teams with highly collaborative people typically have positive relationships and higher levels of employee engagement. Typical behaviours contributing to engagement include helping each other (no brainer here), suggesting new approaches to solving problems and laughing together. Yep – laughing together.

Here are a few examples of these behaviours.

Everyone is very into helping... So, if you go to talk to them they will stop whatever and they shouldn't do that – but they will stop and help. Lim

Everyone just tends to ... because we're a relatively small

team, everyone just tends to stand up and go: Does anyone know anything about this? Or: Can someone help me with this? Someone will put their hand up, so I don't think you need to be in a meeting or anything to see that sort of atmosphere. As I say, just standing there, any time of the day. Kylie

So, if someone's doing something new that the client's asked for, they're looking at a different way of doing things or a different question … But often you'll just sort of look over someone's shoulder and see them do something and go: Hang on. I haven't seen that. What was that? That kind of thing. But, yeah, I mean everyone comes up with new stuff all the time. John

For some of those I interviewed, the collaboration is the result of deep friendships within the team. For these people their colleagues are not only friends but are Facebook friends and they see each other outside of work as well as during office hours.

For others the collaboration is a result of respecting each other's technical skills rather than because they are friends. So, the relationships may be different but the collaborative behaviours are the same.

For you, helping others can be hard to achieve when you have a stack of things on your to-do list. You don't need to allow yourself to be constantly interrupted – you might want to put on some headphones to signal that now is not a good time. Your team will recognise that you need to get something done now and know that you will help them at a time that suits you.

A more cooperative team supports higher learning which, as mentioned before, also contributes to engagement. These characteristics build on each other creating a sense of community within your team.

So, placing all the chocolates on one plate …

To DO

- Help others.
- Encourage informal discussions and joking in the workplace by modelling these behaviours yourself. (However be sensitive to respectful jokes where individuals are not at the centre of ridicule, or flippant remarks.)
- Encourage your team to help each other.
- Take time as a team to analyse learning and discuss new ideas/proposals.

To AVOID

- Being so busy that you can't stop to help others. The gift of a large organisation is that there are many people working to help the organisation to succeed. Don't forget this.

- Seeing the 'people side' of your role as less important to the technical aspects.

12

Relationships matter (but to some more than others)

Closeness to others in the team varied across the five teams, as did the importance of close relationships. In some teams employees felt a greater engagement towards their job or their profession than towards their colleagues; in other teams the relationships were mixed:

Some of the younger guys who I am very good mates with, then there's some people who are just work colleagues who I wouldn't necessarily catch up with outside of work. There are some people who you have a lot of respect for but – not necessarily people you [voice trails off] … So, a very wide range of people – like being at school really. People who you get along with and people who you don't get along with. Wallace

In other teams, having close relationships with colleagues was equally or more important than the work they did. These comments give you a sense of how employees felt about working in their team:

And I think especially working here for so long – some of the people here have been here since I started, and it's I think part of your life. Which I didn't really realise until I wasn't here, and I'm so glad to be back at work (laughs). So, yeah, the people bring the best out of me. Morgan

We usually have a good chat in the morning – we do get in trouble for chatting too much. But, we usually... there's about a group of four or five of us that go to lunch together and sometimes we do try to, when we can all get a chance to meet outside of work, we usually try and take it. Louise

For this team close friendships at work are highly valued. They clearly look forward to coming to work because their friends are there. It makes everything, including a job that does not have the core engaging qualities, easier to do.

These are interesting findings and reflect one of the questions on Gallup's well known Employee Engagement Survey, 'Q12: I have a best friend at work'. While clearly employees have different views about the value of close friendships in the workplace, you as a manager can create an environment with more opportunities for the development of positive relationships.

A few thoughts about putting all the cupcakes on the cake tower …

To DO

- Ensure that the physical environment provides opportunity for people to bump into each other, chat informally and develop relationships.
- Foster informal chatter at the beginning of team meetings whether face-to-face, by telephone or over synchronous communication: show your human side.
- Ask yourself, 'How many times today have I done something that will deepen the relationship that I have with a team member?'

To AVOID

- Spending hours locked away in your office. This will limit your ability to spend time informally with your team and develop deeper relationships.
- Not taking time out for informal banter.
- Being so busy that you can't stop to help others. I know that this means balancing achievement of your own objectives versus helping others.

13

Openness, trust and feeling safe create a great team climate

Team climate is like the weather. You can't always see it, but you can feel it. And sometimes you can tell when there's a storm brewing.

How you feel working in a team is based on the team climate, which in turn is based on how everyone behaves towards each other. In teams with a supportive climate, team members trust each other and 'have each other's back'. In short 'they feel safe'.

People need to feel safe if they are to offer a contrary view, challenge the status quo or experiment with new ideas. If they are feeling nervous and cautious they will only do things the way that they have always been done. As a manager and coach your goal should be to create a work environment where people feel safe to disagree, to try new things and where failure is considered an essential part of learning. This is where the magic and innovation thrive.

Challenging work is the employee-engagement driver for many people. Doing things differently is often required for challenging work. If you want to support an engaged team and to foster creativity and innovation you will need to make it safe to express alternate views – and to fail.

So how do you 'make it safe'? Well, your behaviour is critical as the team will take their lead from you. Create a team habit of sharing learning, 'burnt toast and all'. Being open with your team members should be the norm.

Trust and openness in a team go together like jam and cream on a scone. They complement each other perfectly. Trust helps to create a sense of community, which in turn supports engagement. Not feeling safe and not trusting your colleagues have the opposite effect.

Here are a few comments employees made about the climate in their team, highlighting how it feels to be in a supportive team – or one that is not:

I think when people are joking around with each other and feel free to, you know, if someone's made a mistake they'll just go: Oh, you've done that wrong. I think everyone's really happy when no-one seems to be protecting their own job by worrying about if they're making a mistake or asking a stupid question. Morgan

And then I am so scared of someone finding a mistake because I feel that instead of everyone helping, they are just looking to find a mistake in everyone else's job. Camille

As a leader, listen deeply and model trust and openness. Here's an example of what a leader who listens to their team members does:

They'll always listen to you. And then they'll always come back with: Well, yeah that's a good idea, or: No, because we've tried that already before. If you want to try it again you can, it's up to you. But we have tried it before and it hasn't worked, you know that sort of thing. Kylie

Team members pick up these behaviours and supportive messages by the manager. If they see the manager being open to new ideas they will follow their lead.

A few pointers on creating an open and trusting team environment …

To DO

- Challenge team members to think and do things differently.

- Encourage experimentation.
- Be open to new ideas. This means knowing when to be silent. Hold your opinion until after you have heard what others think.
- Accept any team member's errors or failures. And confess yours. Use the opportunity as a learning moment not a blaming moment and encourage others to do the same.
- Be reliable. Be the person others can count on.
- Discuss learning as a regular part of team meetings.
- Provide boundaries for risk management so possible failure can be contained within parameters acceptable to the team or organisation. For example, *we will only spend this much time or this amount of money trialling this new idea.*
- Show members how to express a different opinion while being respectful. This is a biggie!

To AVOID

- Openly criticising team members.
- Punishing those who fail – through sharp words or actions – or by being silent and ignoring them.
- Expressing your opinion early before you have really asked anyone else. Team members may not feel confident to challenge your view.

14

Team processes provide learning and recognition opportunities

I sat in on a few meetings so I could gain insight into how different teams worked together. Meetings had different objectives and processes but typically were designed to improve visibility on what everyone was working on, and to discuss what was coming up.

Many meetings had a clear focus on learning and recognition. Those meetings with a focus on learning and in which all team members were invited to speak, energised everyone and contributed to engagement.

I suppose we bounce ideas off each other and say: Do

you have this problem when doing this? Is there any way ...? Has anyone thought of ...? Have you got that problem and how did you cope with that? And then I suppose then we implement things. It's really from discussion that changes occur. Marie

Meetings could include a general business update, an around the table opportunity for each team member to provide information or raise questions related to current or planned projects or other organisational issues. One team always included the presentation of a short case study followed by an analysis of lessons learned. In one meeting, a team member was recognised for achieving chartered engineering status. They received their certificate, congratulations from the team manager and an enthusiastic round of applause. Many meetings had instances of joking and laughter. This created a good vibe. This is how one manager organises her team meeting:

What we do is we go through everybody's workloads – we have a discussion around what are you working on and do you have any challenges ... Generally, whatever is happening in the business and what comes out of the leadership team meeting. I try to pass that information to them as much as I can. Cathy

Sharing as much information as you can about the organisation as a whole helps people make connections between what they do every day and where the business is heading. This builds engagement to the job and connection to the company.

Key takeaways on making team meetings a good experience for all …

To DO

- Use meetings as an opportunity to let the team know what is happening in the business.
- Ensure everyone has the opportunity to give an update and to raise questions.
- Encourage team members to bounce ideas off each other.
- Listen to others and provide support for ideas.
- Explore lessons learned from recent projects.
- Give formal recognition to team members.
- Encourage informal banter and laughter.

To AVOID

- Doing all the talking – expressing an opinion too early without space for the ideas of others.
- Being on your phone or laptop during the meeting – a big No No.

15

'Ground control to Major Tom' – How to engage remote teams

All the examples so far have come from teams that spend some if not all of their time together in the same physical location. When you are physically located together there are many opportunities for serendipitous conversations, joking and collaboration. However some teams were physically remote from each other.

Virtual teams benefit from different types of communication which can assist employees develop relationships that help get things done and positively influence engagement. These employees typically use instant messaging, video calls and the good old-fashioned telephone to communicate. While these channels are helpful some loss in communication will occur because of limited face-to-face signals and less time with informal chatter.

Several teams in my study had members geographically dispersed. For them it was important to pay attention to how and how often they communicated with team members who weren't in the building.

One of these teams had a dedicated meeting room with video conference facilities so that team members in both locations could see each other during meetings. I noted that all calls started with informal banter and joking. It felt like everyone was in the same room when I sat in on the video linkups. This team held meetings across sites at least once a week. Another team relied more on online chatting facilities:

We try to catch up weekly. We have a LYNC meeting … We dial in – but it's just through the computer. Like a teleconference – with no visuals – but I can share my screen. We are across three locations – we tend to just jump on the phone which works pretty easily. What we do is we go through everybody's workloads – we have a discussion around what you are working on and do you have any challenges. Cathy

Even though there was no face-to-face communication

with colleagues at other sites, there was a culture of spontaneity and of ensuring that everyone was included in the conversation. Making sure that everyone is involved is even more important when the team cannot see each other.

The reality of the modern working life in organisations is that teams will often be geographically separated. Consideration will need to be given to creating opportunities for team members to connect and develop relationships. When relationships are stronger it follows that there are better conditions for engagement to flourish.

Drum roll please.

The wrap on having great communication between 'Ground control and Major Tom' …

To DO

- Spend more time than usual engaging in informal discussions with colleagues at the beginning of a meeting.
- Use all the channels of communication available to you, recognising that those that provide more face-to-face interaction are richer in quality of interaction – which helps support engagement.
- Create opportunities for the team to relax together.
- Schedule a physical face-to-face meeting at least once a year.

To AVOID

- Communicating only by email. Big mistake. Very boring. Pick up the phone more often.
- Being judgemental when something hasn't been delivered as planned. Make sure you understand the 'Why' or the back story before passing judgement.

*

So, before we have another slice of something delicious, let's review the good stuff on teams and how they influence engagement.

We've chatted about how important it is that everybody helps each other. A bit of a no-brainer this one. While some people will develop close relationships with their colleagues, others will be happy to help but will probably want to keep a bit of distance. Absolutely cool. You can use your normal meeting habits to ensure that everyone is involved. The important thing is openness and trust and everyone feeling safe enough so they can speak their mind.

You may have noticed that I have referred to your role not only as a manager, but also as a coach and leader. These three elements are all part of the same triple layered chocolate cake. And they all contribute to engagement. More on these elements in the next slice of the book.

THE BEST MANAGERS

As a manager, and more importantly as a leader and coach, you are in the 'empowering others' business. As a result your behaviour matters because it directly affects your team members' engagement or disengagement, as the case may be. Positive managerial behaviours that directly influence engagement include:

- giving staff freedom to act
- offering support and asking staff what they need to succeed
- providing recognition
- laughing with the team and engaging in informal 'chit chat'
- demonstrating an openness to new ideas
- providing a safe environment where people can express contrary views
- showing a concern for work/life balance.

Behaviours that influence employee engagement negatively include micro-managing staff and being confrontational.

A few reflections on these important behaviours are next on the menu.

16

Be open to new ideas

There can be tension between doing things efficiently and doing things differently. Innovation can spring from a problem, an emerging opportunity or simply from a desire to do things in another way. While we know that many new ideas fail, if we always do things the way we always have we miss opportunities to learn and develop. In a rapidly changing world it's important to explore new ideas as they are often a source of competitive advantage.

As a leader your openness to new ideas influences how open your team will be. Simply put they will take their cues from you. I recognise that it can be hard to be open to new ideas when you are under pressure to deliver:

But you know, when the pressure is on – you still need to think of the ideas to make it not so pressure filled. Cathy

Showing an openness to new ideas is as much about what you say as what you do. So, listen deeply. Be aware of your body language. An eye roll, a click of a pen, a glance at your phone or a sigh can be fatal for a new idea.

As a leader the bottom line is that there are hidden treasures to be found when you are open to new ideas.

To DO

- *Stating the obvious* – be open to new ideas.
- Create opportunities for team members to share their new ideas.
- Non-judgementally accept any team member's errors or failures. Convert failures into a learning moment and encourage others to do the same.

To AVOID

- Openly criticising team members or making them feel inadequate if an initiative fails.

17

Offer support first and advice second

During my research I sat in on a number of meetings and had the opportunity to observe how managers support their team. The most effective managers would ensure that everyone was involved in the discussion. They gave each team member time to talk about their projects and challenges followed by a discussion around how these challenges could be addressed.

The best managers encouraged their staff to identify potential solutions to their challenges, calling on other team members to offer views and support as well. This was great role modelling.

As a manager, and particularly if you have been

promoted up through the ranks, you might be tempted to share what you know when an employee asks because – well obviously – you know the answer. You need to pause here. While you may be a technical expert you are also a manager and more importantly a 'coach'. The distinction here is important: as a coach the best way to help others is to give them the opportunity to solve the problem themselves. It is very tempting to be the 'all knowing' technical expert and share your infinite wisdom.

When you are asked how to solve a problem, pose a few questions to help the employee think through their options, possible outcomes and implications. Once they have decided then offer support in implementing their decision.

The wrap-up …

To DO

• Listen. And listen deeply for every word being said and those that might be unsaid.

• Ask questions that will help your employee solve the problem for themselves.

• Let your employee report on their activities and challenges – without interruption.

• Explore together their options and likely outcomes.

• Probe as to which option is their preferred one and why.

- Resist the urge to recommend a solution.
- Offer support for the next steps.

To AVOID

- Being impatient.
- Blurting out your preferred direction.

18

Take time out to analyse lessons learned

It's easy to rush from project to project without taking time to pause, reflect and capture learning. We often deliver several projects simultaneously. Because of these multiple demands and related time pressure, it's tempting to skip the learning stages. But we lose a lot when we do this.

It's important to take time out to analyse lessons learned. Specifically, what worked well and what didn't. This learning will help us to manage similar projects more effectively in the future. Once you have identified learning get it written down and saved. Make sure the team knows where these notes are stored and refer to them during the planning stages of future projects.

One of the teams I observed had a 'lessons learned' spot as a standard part of their weekly meeting. Each team member took turns at presenting an incident or case study with a focus on lessons learned, followed by a facilitated discussion.

And the benefits? The team created a learning habit incorporating analysis, reflection and discussion. The team was energised as they explored the learning, creating a stronger connection between participants. The rotating facilitating role provided a leadership opportunity which was a valuable learning experience. (Remember our previous chat about how learning and mastering skills is a wonderful and empowering thing.)

And again – a quick wrap …

To DO

- Encourage analysis and reflection in your conversations with your team.
- Plan milestone or project reviews to capture learning.
- Make sure these reflective milestones happen.
- Record learnings and reflect on them for future projects.

To AVOID

- Skipping the recommendations above.

19

Be fair and consistent

As a manager you make many decisions about your team. These could be about salary or benefits, who gets promoted (or who doesn't), participation in new projects, attendance at development activities or simpler things, like who sits next to the window. I can remember when I worked in a large organisation that there could be grief around who was invited to a meeting at the company's head office at times when there weren't enough funds for everyone to go. Going to the meeting was not only a measure of your status but also provided a valuable networking opportunity.

So those who weren't invited felt they were missing out. They felt less valued.

So here's the key message to remember. The decisions

you make will be observed and judged. If the decisions are not perceived to be fair and consistent, they will have a direct bearing on engagement – and not in a good way. The knock-on impact could include withdrawal from participation in activities, not giving their best, or beginning to search for another role. It could also influence team cohesion.

It's important to look at your decisions through a lens of fairness, inclusion and equity. If you think that a decision may be misunderstood, make a point of explaining the rationale in a team meeting or by speaking directly to those who may be slighted by the decision. Don't play favourites. The time you spend with each individual will have a bearing on how they perceive their value, through you, to the organisation.

Feelings of unfairness can linger below the surface for a long time and have a negative influence on the trust you've built, trust that is important in any team.

Pulling it all together …

To DO

• Always consider the impact of a decision from a fairness and consistency perspective.
• When you make a decision that may be perceived as unfair take time to explain why it was made.
• If you are not sure how to approach a situation that

might be perceived inequitably, seek out counsel from a colleague or mentor.

To AVOID

- Treating members of your team differently. Favouritism does not support engagement.
- Rushing a decision without having thought through the consequences.

20

Celebrate the team's differences

Diversity adds dynamism to a team. Different perspectives reveal new information, promote divergent thinking and encourage exploration of ideas. Often the greater your team's diversity, the better your capacity to understand the diversity of your customers' perspectives and needs, whether they be inside or outside the organisation. Diversity was highly valued in the company where I undertook my research. Listen to John's remark on his first day at work:

I do remember the very first desk where I sat. There were four people around me and each person was born on a different continent, which I thought was kind of cool. John

Now, diversity could relate to experience, gender, age, nationality, thinking style, personality, or football team supported. And hey, I'm just getting started. To build a diverse team you need to consciously recruit for it or you will end up building a team of clones – people just like you. We must consciously disrupt our very human tendency of seeing value in people like us. When this happens, and it is very common, we miss all the good stuff that difference in thinking style and experience brings.

While decision making processes take longer when there are more voices, everyone will benefit from the diverse perspectives. The last thing any team needs is *group think*, because you will always do things the way you always have.

So, how can you leverage the smorgasbord of goodies that your diverse team brings? Here's a few ideas.

Invite your team members to share their unique work and or life perspectives. For example, if your company is running a project in an interesting geographical location, arrange for a briefing about the project followed by delightful nibbles from that region. It will add to everyone's knowledge about the project, enhance understanding of a different culture and provide a wonderful opportunity for informal chatter and networking. Celebrate your team member's national day, or ask them to bring in a cultural artefact and explain its importance in their culture.

So bringing together these different canapes ...

To DO

• Actively recruit employees with a diversity of life experience and cultural socialisation.

• Take a hard line to recruiting for 'fit' where this is used to screen out diversity. Ensure a focus on 'complementarity' to broaden opportunities for people who have different backgrounds, experiences, industry knowledge, etc.

• Think about who your customers are and mirror this breadth in your team make up.

• Tap into this richness of perspective during team meetings and in your individual discussions.

• Hold an event where a team member from a different culture cooks a traditional meal and shares learning from their unique upbringing.

To AVOID

• Recruiting people just like yourself.

• Not seeking to learn from others who are diverse from you.

21

Laugh out loud

It's great to hear laughter. Laughter brings levity, builds community and positively influences well-being. Think about the last time you laughed out loud and how it made you feel. I guarantee it was an experience that you looked forward to repeating.

During my research I heard laughter a lot: in team meetings, in the corridors and during our interviews. Indeed, when I reviewed my thesis, I found 12 mentions of people laughing when they were answering questions in the interview. (This was not the intended purpose of the question). In some cultures, laughing and working are like water and oil: they are not perceived to mix. But this is not what I found in my study nor what I have personally experienced in great workplaces.

The presence or absence of laughter provides insight into a person's mood and their feelings of engagement – even if this engagement is related to the other people they are laughing with.

I conducted my research in the Australian office of an international company. Here are a few examples of managers talking about their team culture and processes that encourage laughter.

They are a lot of fun and 'taking the Mickey' out of each other making jokes. It's hard to offend them. Max

I think that you need to have some general chit chat – you know – they are still working but we sit close enough – so that we can all still have a bit of a chit chat or a laugh or something that I think in itself is stimulating as well. Because otherwise you just sit there on the computer and … I don't find that to be a good working environment. Alice

Laughter (the laughter when everyone laughs together) will enhance positive feelings between team members, which in turn will support collaboration. And I've already mentioned the tremendous value of your team supporting each other and 'having each other's back'.

A few ideas to promote fun, playfulness and laughter …

To DO

- Reflect on how often you hear laughter in team meetings and the circumstances that prompt this.
- Take action to create more of these circumstances.
- Use humour with internal communications.
- Create time at the beginning of your team meetings for informal chatter and joking.
- Build playful spaces in your physical work environment where people can relax together.
- Smile often – it's a great start.

To AVOID

- Only talking about business. Boring.

22

Share the big picture

It's easy to feel lost in a large organisation and not understand how your daily activities contribute to the organisation's success. As a leader you help your team make these connections by sharing the big picture about where the company is going and what it means for them. Even if there are company newsletters or other channels it's useful for you to share the news as well. Remember, it's hard to overcommunicate.

Picture this: your company is about to buy another company or to reorganise. I know that sometimes you may not know if or how your team will be affected. At these times, admitting you don't know is a great way of being open and authentic. Use these opportunities to reach out to your leaders with these questions and then brief the team on what you learn from them.

Great managers share company news on a regular basis and welcome questions. The discussion process helps team members to feel more connected to the organisation – which is another level of engagement we will discuss later.

Bringing it together …

To DO

• Tell everyone what's going on in the business. Share as much as you can.

• Schedule an update on company news in your fortnightly or monthly team meeting.

• Give your team plenty of opportunities to ask questions.

• If you don't know the answer to their questions – admit it – and commit to finding out the answer and reporting back.

To AVOID

• Not communicating what's going on, particularly during periods of significant change.

23

Say thank you

You know, we don't say thank you nearly as often as we think we do. Stop and reflect. How many times have you said thank you to someone today? These two words of gratitude have motivational power. They let the other person know that they and their actions are appreciated, and spur them on to continue behaving in this way. While saying thank you has magic, this power is enhanced if you add specific details to the feedback. Perhaps like this:

'When you stepped in to help Franc with the backlog of work you demonstrated that you had his back. This was valued by Franc and set a great example for other team members.'

Saying thank you is appreciated by everyone. It's a simple form of recognition that strengthens relationships and enhances a person's engagement. I remember being given a beautiful arrangement of flowers by my boss after I had facilitated a workshop. Totally unexpected as I had loved pulling the workshop together and was just doing my job. I felt so appreciated by this surprise thank you that I never forgot how it felt.

Recapping the cream on the pavlova …

To DO

- Say thank you and be specific about what you are thanking people for.
- Think of other ways to say thank you – perhaps via an email or a bunch of flowers.
- Be specific to let them know exactly how they have added value.

To AVOID

- The obvious – not taking the time to say thank you.
- Being general in your thanks i.e. 'Thanks for your help this week'. Is this conveying the behaviour you appreciated and would they know which aspect to repeat?

*

Pulling together the learning from this slice, you will be a better leader, manager and coach when you let everyone know how what they do contributes to the company's success; you model a genuine interest in new ideas; you encourage your team members to find solutions to their own challenges (and hold back on offering your own opinion); you take time out to identify and capture learning; you are fair and consistent when you make decisions; you laugh out loud, and always saying thank you. Phew!

Now, let's have a peek at those things on the organisational buffet which also influence engagement.

BIG
ORGANISATIONS

I t's easy to get lost in a big organisation. There are systems and processes quite apart from a huge spider's web of an organisational chart to navigate. How you feel about who you are in a large organisation is influenced by the team you work in and how you perceive your identity and status in the hierarchy.

When we choose to work for a large organisation our sense of identity is very much associated with the organisation's brand. I want to explore this a bit as engagement does not just relate to the work we do or the team we're in, but is also influenced by our sense of connection to the organisation and who we think we are inside the organisation.

24

Who am I?
Influence of status and
identity on engagement

❋

'Who am I?'
I think about this question when I'm applying for a new job and I need to mentally ready myself for the inevitable questions around who I am and what I have achieved. I know my responses will reflect my strengths, my values and how I perceive myself.

When I'm asked why I want this job in this organisation I will reveal how important the brand and status of the organisation are to me. For some people having a close alignment with the objectives, values and brand of the organisation is important. For others, less so.

While a company's brand is visible in advertising and on the web, the status and identity of roles and teams are not always so discernible from the outside. But the signs are there once you start working in the company. You will hear conversations that provide clues as to which roles and teams are sexy and on the 'up and up', and which roles and teams are not. Employees quickly develop a sense of who they are in the organisation and how important their role and team are. Their sense of identity and status influences feelings of self-worth.

All organisations have a hierarchy or status typically related to seniority and profession. In hospitals for example, doctors are at the top of the totem pole and there is an additional status ladder related to specialisation within this population. In engineering firms, it's not surprising that the engineers dominate. This was the reality at the organisation where I undertook my research.

Of the five teams I investigated three teams provided engineering services that were billable to clients, while the other two were classified as non-billable or 'indirect' functions such as finance or marketing. The term 'indirect' appeared to have a pejorative meaning – which in layman's language was that their roles were considered less important than the engineering roles directly funding the business. Several comments made by those in non-billable roles revealed feelings of not being as valued.

This sense of being less valued appeared to have an indirect impact on their engagement, but to a lesser extent than other characteristics. So, it mattered a bit (and managers need to recognise this) but not as much as characteristics related to the job itself, professional identity and the feeling of connection to the team.

So, what's the learning here for you as manager? Well you are trying to achieve a winning formula – with your employees loving their job, feeling valued, appreciating their team environment and feeling connected to the organisation. You have the power to influence the first two areas and I've given you suggestions in previous chapters on things you can do. Your messages around your team members being valued will affect their status and identity. While organisational cultural factors are further away from you it is still possible to influence them.

A few reflections on things you can do to help your team members have a stronger sense of identity and connection to the organisation follow.

To DO

- Help your team understand how they contribute to the organisation's success in tangible ways.
- Make comments that reinforce how important their role is.

- Undertake activities to define the team's values and identity.
- Celebrate success together.

To AVOID

- Making remarks that make team members feel they are in a less valued role.
- Focusing on the things that separate teams, functions and divisions and treating these units as 'the enemy within'.

25

Feeling connected to the organisation

So many factors influence feeling connected to the organisation: its leadership team, its culture and its values, to name but a few. It's highly unlikely that everyone in the organisation will feel the same connection to the organisation. And that's fine.

People have different motivations for working: for some having a strong connection to the organisation is not a priority. Some people I interviewed felt more connected to their professional discipline or team than to the organisation.

As a manager you want to ensure that your team is engaged so that they give their best, enjoy the work and stay and contribute longer. You can play a role in deepening their connection to the organisation by letting people know what is going on in the business and answering their questions - making the linkages more obvious between the work of your team and the bigger goals and strategy of the organisation.

However, there may be times of uncertainty. In the organisation where I undertook my research, the industry had been going through a downturn and there had been layoffs. This had unsettled those I spoke with and although many were still fond of the organisation their connection had weakened. Many reported that during times of uncertainty, communication had dropped off.

Over the last two years – what has happened is that as the business has gone down and down and down – the level of engagement and communication from our strong leaders – who needed to give us a call to action and lead us – like – the times are bad – but we are going to get through that. They just went to ground. Sally

As this comment reveals, at these times communication was considered even more important.

I've touched on the importance of culture a couple of times. Culture covers many aspects of life in an organisation and is often most visible when you first join an organisation. It's useful to talk about culture with your team. You can lead conversations around how culture influences attitudes and behaviour in the organisation. Your team will be particularly interested in which behaviours are most important for success.

I'm always surprised when people identify organisational culture as something separate from their own behaviour. Every day, our conversations and emails contribute to everyone else's perception of culture.

Remind your team that they play an important role in building the culture and in making the organisation a great place to work.

To DO

- Communicate often and more frequently during times of uncertainty.
- Discuss 'What's it like to work here?' and what this means for our behaviour.
- Explore the values that are most important to the team.
- Remind the team that their daily behaviours build the culture of the team and the organisation.
- Recognise that not all team members may feel deeply connected to the organisation.

To AVOID

• Worrying if team members display a stronger connection to their professional discipline or the team than to the organisation.

26

Gotta get balance – Is it possible to have your cake and eat it too?

❋

It can be hard to achieve the right balance between time at work and time at home. We may want to invest more time in both but there are only 24 hours in the day.

When you work too long and get weary you are not at your best in the office nor when you get home. You gotta get balance and as a manager you need to help your team to achieve this too. Having balance is a core condition in which employee engagement can happen, rather than being a driver in itself. It's a bit like you'll enjoy your cake a lot more if it is served on a sparkling clean plate.

One of the questions I asked in my study was 'What's it like to work here?' I received responses such as *very friendly*, with a positive *family feel* and *respectful of work/life balance*. Indeed, the importance of family and achieving a good work/life balance came through strongly. Here are some of the things they told me, starting with messages received on arrival in the organisation.

The first week we received the orientation with the company. They told you everything from how do you work – like you should have a balance in work and life. Morris

I heard several examples of managers encouraging team members to go home at the end of the day.

Normally – sometimes we work a longer time in the day because of the urgent part of the work, and then maybe we can stay longer. But normally it's not urgent and still in the plan. Our manager asks us to leave on time because we have the family. Lionel

From a practical level it makes sense to stop working when you are tired. A reflection from one of the managers about problems associated with working late:

I always tell them not to work too late because they get tired and you make more mistakes. Then you need to spend the following day to clean up those mistakes. So I say that the moment you feel tired – you should stop and go home.

And also if it's late, to grab a taxi and go home and have a rest. John

There has been a lot of discussion about the need for organisations to ensure that employees have work/life balance if they are to be at their best. A part of achieving work/life balance is around being flexible about when people arrive and leave and where they work from. There's a multitude of options you can explore with your team, and trust sits at the core of this important element.

To DO

- Trust your people.
- Be flexible about working times and locations.
- Be aware of people working late and discuss this with them.
- Offer support to rebalance their work load if this is the problem.
- Be a role model in achieving work/life balance and work flexibly to normalise the practice.

To AVOID

- Working all the time, which sets the expectation that your team should do the same.
- Glorifying those who stay late in the office.
- Being selective and inconsistent with who gets to work flexibly.

27

Moods, motivations and trade-offs

I've talked a lot about how jobs, teams and your behaviour as a manager influence employee engagement. What I haven't talked about is the people. And this is a biggie! The people in your team have different moods, motivations, personalities and circumstances – and not surprisingly, these factors influence engagement.

At different times in our life and career we will have different motivations. For example, while autonomy to decide how work is undertaken is widely recognised as contributing to engagement, when we're new in our career we accept that we need to receive a lot of direction. Similarly, if we have just returned to work following a break for maternity leave or a major illness, we may be content to undertake more routine, rather than challenging, work until we're back into the swing of things.

A few of the people I spoke with discussed trade-offs when we talked about those times when they were most engaged. For example, being in a supportive team was a good trade-off for having a job without variety or challenge. For others, working in a project that built their skills was a good compromise for working in a team that had conflictual behaviours.

The reality is that our moods, motivations and trade-offs affect our work and life. Great managers appreciate this reality. Having regular conversations with your team around how they are going, asking if they are OK and being flexible about work arrangements are all great ways to support them.

Here's how you can help …

To DO

- Be sensitive to the influence of life circumstances on your team's motivation and capacity to work at their optimum.
- If you sense a drop in energy or motivation, talk to them about it.
- Be flexible with work arrangements, particularly after a return to work from a long break.

To AVOID

- Making assumptions about why someone may appear less motivated than usual.

WHAT IT ALL MEANS

You're now up to the final part of the book where we nibble on some final cake crumbs and I pull the learning together.

28

Pulling it all together

G reat. You've made it here. Well done. (Cue for a song. I choose *Cake By the Ocean*).

I know I've shared a lot about what influences engagement, so I wanted to do a wrap of the main messages so far.

Firstly, engagement is complex. We understand many of the things that drive engagement relate to the job, team environment and behaviour of the manager. The importance of these things will vary for each employee depending on what's going on in their life at any particular time.

It's also valuable to remember that our thoughts about the organisation, its business activities, objectives, values, culture and what we think of the leadership team will influence our feelings of attachment to the organisation.

At a more personal level, how your employees perceive the role they undertake and the status of the team may also influence their sense of identity and engagement. Your employees may not share the same level of connectedness to their job, to the team or to the organisation.

So the wrap, the things that absolutely, deliciously and positively influence employee engagement:

- jobs which have interesting challenges and problems to solve; with freedom to determine how to achieve objectives; opportunity to achieve things – even little things; potential for learning; and being so busy that time flies by

- a team environment that has ingredients of trust, feeling safe, lots of collaboration and positive relationships

- team meetings which bind everyone together by stimulating learning, providing recognition opportunities and encouraging laughter

- managers who provide a high level of autonomy; are open to new ideas; are fair, inclusive and consistent; offer support first and advice second; give recognition; say thank you; take time to engage in informal chit-chat and joking; and enable their team members to achieve work/life balance.

Big organisations can be hard to navigate and it's easy

to feel lost. Helping your team members understand the direction of the business and the role they play in contributing to its success is one of your responsibilities.

Remember – you are not just a manager: you are also a leader and a coach. You have an important role to play in motivating and guiding others.

Now would be a great time to get another coffee and to open a notebook, (an iPad's fine as well), and to jot down any new insights into managing and engaging your team.

29

Wisdom from HR practitioners

To help me write this book, I asked human resource colleagues their learning from running big employee-engagement programs. Their insights were valuable and complimented the data I collected through my PhD research and from my own experience. Their comments reinforced many of the observations already made and are particularly helpful for those who have responsibility for organisational wide employee engagement initiatives.

Employee engagement programs typically involve employee surveys, communication activities and action planning. They aim to identify where changes can be made to improve employee engagement and to facilitate positive change. It's also hoped that as engagement increases so too will business performance.

Human resource practitioners and corporate communication teams typically carry responsibility for delivery of employee engagement programs. Because of this I was interested in learning from my colleagues:

1. What their understanding of employee engagement was
2. What factors most contributed to employee engagement
3. What were the biggest drivers of disengagement
4. What were the biggest obstacles to increasing engagement in the workplace
5. What support or resources, if any, were critical for success
6. If they had to do it again ('it' being a large engagement program) what they would do differently
7. What most influenced their own engagement.

Here's what they told me…

1. What is employee engagement?

There isn't agreement about employee engagement.
Some felt that it was the connection between the employee and the organisation; a measure of the extent to which an employee believes in the purpose of the organisation and its strategies. Central to this was an employee's

understanding of how they contribute to the vision, and being motivated to support this vision. One respondent described feeling committed to the organisation as an indicator of engagement.

Another colleague declared they weren't a fan of the term and observed that no one had worked out what employee engagement was, adding that they did not feel that the term added anything more to what was already known about intrinsic motivation. This sentiment is reflected in the academic literature with suggestions that employee engagement is a repackaging of older concepts such as job satisfaction and organisational commitment, also drawing heavily on Bandura's work on self-efficacy. (Self-efficacy refers to an individual's belief in their capacity to execute behaviours necessary to produce specific performance outcomes, Bandura, 1977.)

It's a two-way process.

Others described employee engagement as a two-way process, where there is genuine and meaningful communication and alignment between an individual's values and those of the organisation. Employees feel that they belong with their personal identity intrinsically connected to the organisation. However, this relationship is fluid and subject to change.

Positive feelings and behaviours are a sign.

When employees are engaged they typically apply

discretionary effort and are more productive. At the same time they experience a sense of joy and satisfaction in their work. Being engaged was also described as a time when employees' hearts and minds were invested in their work.

Can be a full or partial experience.

Engagement is not an 'on or off' experience. An individual can be engaged in a task, say if it's highly stimulating, while at the same time not feeling a sense of engagement towards the organisation. Similarly, employees may feel a strong sense of attachment to their local work unit with lesser feelings of connection towards the organisation.

2. What factors contribute most to employee engagement?

Respect

Being respected for one's contribution. Respect was directly aligned with feeling valued.

Trust

A work culture that is built on trust and autonomy, leaving people free to determine how they will achieve their work objectives. Without trust, employees see engagement activities as 'lip service'.

Trust comes from a mutual respect and a strong psychological 'contract' between the parties.

How an employee is managed on a day to day basis will have a bearing on trust, as well as how inclusive the organisation is to work for.

Clear Strategy

The starting point is a well-articulated strategy that makes sense. Without a clear strategy and excellent leaders, it's difficult to achieve employee engagement – even if you have world class HR professionals, programs and systems.

Leadership

Leaders being open, transparent and authentic is key. Few things require leadership secrecy.

You need the best leaders possible particularly in senior roles. Leaders articulate strategy, motivate teams and stretch them to achieve their goals.

Leadership includes receiving candid and constructive feedback and ensuring it's responded to.

Working for a successful organisation

For some working with a successful organisation or believing that the organisation can be successful is important, impacting directly on their sense of identity.

One size does not fit all

One size does not fit all and individuals will be motivated by different factors. These factors shift as we age and mature.

Using their skills

Employees want to use their skills and knowledge. They also want to try new things and risk failing, without repercussions.

Being recognised

Employees feel valued when they are acknowledged for their expertise and contribution.

Being challenged

Being challenged is central to engagement for some. While for others, just doing their job well is enough.

Meaningful work

Doing something I enjoy. Making a meaningful difference.

Appreciation and feedback

Believing that my bosses appreciate my efforts and my contribution.

Learning and progress towards career aspirations

Gaining experience, knowledge, education and/or exposure helps me grow towards my career and life objectives.

Team environment

Enjoying the people I work with.

Relations with my manager

Liking my boss.

'Cool' workplace

Being inspired by my workplace, for example the people and environment. Enjoying the 'cool' factor. This is as relevant for younger workers as for older workers – sometimes more than we realise.

3. *What are the biggest drivers of disengagement at work?*

Poor leadership.

- Being insincere. Not giving a straight answer.
- Not being available.
- Flip-flopping on decisions and inconsistency
- Lack of clarity around vision and strategy.
- Lack of trust in decisions made by senior leaders.
- A sense of not being able to 'make a difference', when 99% of people come to work to make a positive contribution.
- Not having interesting/challenging work to do.
- Not having a sense of ownership or accountability.
- A workplace (and this means managers and colleagues) that does not value an employee's unique talents nor ensures the employee knows how they are contributing.
- A manager who doesn't give you interesting work.
- A manager who doesn't provide coaching, feedback or praise.
- A manager who micromanages.
- 'People join organisations, but they leave bosses'. But leaving doesn't necessarily mean resigning; disengaging is a form of leaving.
- Perceptions that there exists a problem with fairness, equality and parity.
- A culture that lacks trust and is based on fear.

- Having change imposed without consultation.
- Being treated as a resource or a 'number'. This is particularly evident in large organisations.

4. If you have been involved in running a large engagement program, what were the biggest obstacles to increasing employee engagement?

- Poor leadership.
- Too much 'corporate speak'.
- Bad experience with past programs.
- Lack of trust.
- Politics.
- Lack of active sponsorship. 'The music and words need to align.'
- Perception that it was just a data collection exercise from which people's inputs would not make a difference.
- Poor workplace culture with limited respect for individuals.
- Expecting people to leave their 'lives at the door', and where there is more internal competition than is healthy.
- Lack of compelling strategy and a dysfunctional executive team.
- Lack of staff involvement in planning of the initiative to gain an understanding of the program and involvement in implementation.

- Misunderstanding of what engagement is.
- Not understanding that one size does not fit all: the 'sheep dip' approach is a disaster.
- Managers not taking ownership of engagement or dedicating enough resources.
- Leaving it all to HR or internal communications team to implement.

5. *What support or resources are critical for success?*

- Well-considered change and communications planning (knowing the landscape, stakeholders, drivers, etc).
- Having formal and informal conversations. Communicate frequently through a range of channels. Keeping messages simple. A one pager leadership guide or a basic PowerPoint with speaking notes makes it easier for a leader to make messages relevant to the audience.
- Training for leaders.
- Positive leadership role-modelling.
- Holding people accountable for values and behaviours so that it's not just about *what do you do in your job?* but *how you do your job?*
- Establish a forum of key stakeholders to monitor progress and adjust. The ability to measure quickly and easily is important.

- Management following through on what has been promised, and only promising what they can deliver – and having accountability for the outcomes.

6. If you had to do it ('it' being a large engagement program) again, what would you do differently?

- More leadership development to manage the change including executive coaching in 'walking the talk'.
- Good question. Each program will be different so it's a difficult question to answer other than to say I would reflect on what has worked, and what didn't hit the mark.
- I would probably work harder with the Board to ensure that the right CEO was appointed Ultimately, without the right CEO, it's hard to implement sound strategy and motivate good leaders.
- Front-up leader engagement is critical. Getting their buy-in, making them part of the decision-making process goes a long way.
- Engagement programs have tended to focus on the action of running a survey. I think surveys are important in the sense that, if statistically valid, they provide important data to work with. But one common mistake is to spend so much energy on running the survey, then forget to communicate and follow-up with employees. Running a survey allows employees

to have a voice, but if they don't trust the process, or perceive that management isn't doing anything with the feedback, or worse, feel like it's used against them, the program has the opposite of its intended consequence.

• Segmenting and analysing the data to more deeply understand the drivers of engagement and disengagement in different areas of the organisation.

• Teaching managers how to listen and respond to employee feedback. Part of this includes helping them understand that a survey is only one data point, but that they should engage in many different types of feedback gathering, including town halls and one-on-one meetings.

• Move out managers/leaders that don't have what it takes. This can sometimes mean moving a leader out who is getting results (in the short term), despite his employees feeling disengaged.

• Sit down the CEO and be utterly convinced they were doing 'it' for the right reasons. If the CEO does not believe in what they are doing ... no one else will.

7. What things most influence your own engagement?

• Knowing what is happening in the organisation that is relevant to me.

• My sense of alignment with the organisation.

• Workplace culture.

- Being trusted and given autonomy.
- Being accountable.
- Having the opportunity to do my best work.
- Having interesting and challenging work and receiving praise when I get the work done well.
- Undertaking transformational work.
- Leading and developing others so we achieve together.
- How leaders behave. Working with a great CEO, smart colleagues and staff.
- Feeling a sense of connection with my manager and the senior leadership team.
- Working with people from different cultures.

*

I know that this chapter is different from the others. Not unlike having your coffee delivered by the pastry chef, rather than the waiter. Different roles are required to create a great café experience and there are diverse roles supporting employee engagement in a large organisation. It's always useful to hear the different voices.

While the human resources and communication teams may carry responsibility for delivery of organisational wide engagement programs, it is the people leading teams, like you, who have a more direct impact on the engagement of their team members.

30

Why whispering works

I hope you've picked up a few ideas for things you can do to positively influence engagement within your team. And I also hope that you have identified those things which drive your own engagement: deeper personal insights about what gets you fired up each day will help you to be a better leader.

Within these pages, I've presented learning from folks I spoke with in a large international organisation as well as from human resource practitioners across different industries. And of course, my own experience has been infused within the coffee. My overall motivation has been to help you, to help your organisation, to create a great place to work.

In writing this book I was motivated to show a quieter way to lift engagement, focussing on those things within your control as a manager. Take time to reflect on my suggestions (while you enjoy another slice of that triple-layered chocolate cake), and consider which ones you can implement to make a big difference in inspiring your team to give their best.

Based on the learning presented in 'Engagement Whisperer', I have developed a number of templates that you may find useful for talking to your team about what engages them at work. They include a self-assessment template that your employees can complete along with questions to facilitate a chat about engagement. If you would like to receive these by email, go to engagementwhisperer.com and join my mailing list.

I wish you the best.

Warmly,
Tracy

p.s. You can find me on:
Twitter @engagewhisperer
Linkedin https://www.linkedin.com/in/tracystanley1/
…and in all cafes serving great cappuccinos and cake.

p.p.s. I hope you've picked up ideas on things you can do.
And feel inspired to go online and write a review –
after you've finished your coffee and cake of course.

References

Bandura, Albert. Self-efficacy: toward a unifying theory of behavioral change. *Psychological review* 84.2 (1977): 191.

Gallup. 2010. The state of the global workplace: A worldwide study of employee engagement and well-being. 36-36.

Harter, J. K., Schmidt, F. L., & Hayes, T. L. 2002. Business-unit-level relationship between employee satisfaction, employee engagement, and business outcomes: A meta-analysis. *Journal of Applied Psychology*, 87(2): 268-279.

Kahn, W. A. (1990). Psychological conditions of personal engagement and disengagement at work. *Academy of management journal*, 33(4), 692–724.

Macey, W. H., & Schneider, B. 2008. The meaning of employee engagement. *Industrial and Organizational Psychology*, 1(1): 3-30.

May, D. R., Gilson, R. L., & Harter, L. M. 2004. The psychological conditions of meaningfulness, safety and availability and the engagement of the human spirit at work. *Journal of Occupational and Organizational Psychology*, 77(1): 11-37.

Pink, D. H. (2011). *Drive: The surprising truth about what motivates us*. Penguin.

Saks, A. M. 2006. Antecedents and consequences of employee engagement. *Journal of Managerial Psychology*, 21(7): 600-619.

Shuck, B., & Wollard, K. 2010. Employee engagement and HRD: A seminal review of the foundations. *Human Resource Development Review*, 9(1): 89-110.

Stanley, T. (2016). *Work environments, creative behaviours and employee engagement*. (PhD Monograph), Queensland University of Technology.

About Tracy Stanley

I loved the adventures of *The Secret Seven* as a child: a small troupe solving mysteries together, often on their bicycles. Their exploits inspired my career in foreign lands and interest in understanding what makes a great team.

Following a corporate career in human resource management and organisational change working within travel, technology, government, financial services, mining, education and health sectors, I am now an entrepreneur where I write and speak to inspire others.

Always curious, I've collected a few qualifications including an MBA and MBus (Research). In 2016, I completed my doctoral thesis at the Queensland University of Technology, investigating how work environments influence creative behaviours and employee engagement.

I love listening to people with diverse life stories and sharing what I know at conferences and through the occasional blog on LinkedIn.

My friends say that I am imaginative and tenacious, although my husband would hasten to add 'untidy'.